SACRED NATURE

SAFARI
COLOURING BOOK

Jonathan & Angela Scott

Bradt GUIDES

Dedication

To our grandson Michael Jonathan Meek and his generation of conservationists with love.

Foreword

There is no greater adventure than a safari to the Mara-Serengeti in East Africa where Angela and I have spent so many years immersing ourselves in the lives of the great predators – particularly the big cats that bring an exquisite tension to the landscape. This vast ecosystem of 25,000km² includes the Maasai Mara National Reserve in Kenya and adjoining Serengeti National Park in Tanzania. It is home to the "great migration" – the two million wildebeest, zebras and gazelles that criss-cross the grasslands and acacia thickets in their endless search for food and water.

This is a book for everyone to enjoy. We love to draw and hope you will join us on a virtual safari using your imagination to bring the illustrations to life by colouring them. They feature many of the animals and birds that you will see on your travels, as well as the Maasai pastoralists who have roamed these lands for centuries living side by side with the wild animals and relying on their livestock for all their needs. All of the species illustrated can be found among the IUCN's Red List that charts the status of the world's most endangered species. It is our sincere hope that with greater awareness, and your help, none of these amazing creatures will disappear from the planet.

These concerns prompted us to publish *Sacred Nature: Life's Eternal Dance* (HPH, 2016), that celebrates the wonders of the Mara-Serengeti. That book was Angela's vision. It is Angela who has inspired us to find a different, more spiritual way of looking at nature, one that we try to evoke in our photographs and drawings. In 2021 we published *Sacred Nature 2: Reconnecting People to Our Planet* (HPH, 2021). It takes the theme of the first volume and extends it across the globe, focusing on landscapes and the creatures that inhabit them. As Angela says: "If we truly wish to protect elephants and lions, then we must help preserve their natural environment. Give them space to live and they will prosper."

THE SACRED NATURE INITIATIVE

The Sacred Nature books are the flagship for the Sacred Nature Initiative (SNI), a non-profit we founded in 2021 based on three pillars: Inspire, Educate and Conserve. With more than half the world now living in cities or urban areas, people have become disconnected from the vital role that nature plays in all our lives. Many children barely leave their rooms, content to inhabit a "virtual" world rather than venturing into the great outdoors to enjoy its gifts firsthand. We do not own nature, land isn't a commodity to be used as we please, nature is something to be respected and nurtured, held in trust for the benefit of future generations; something sacred. As such, we must plan for the long term, embrace environmental stewardship, look to sustainable practices that promote the provision of clean energy and the equitable use of natural resources.

Though the SNI is global in its scope and ideals, Phase 1 will focus on the place we know best: the Mara-Serengeti ecosystem. By purchasing this book, you will have already supported the SNI as a percentage of the profits from sales will be donated to projects supported by the Initiative.

If you'd like to learn more about SNI and how you can reconnect to nature, please visit: **sacrednatureinitiative.com** and for more on our work: **bigcatpeople.com**.

Lion and lioness.

Male impala and herd of females.

Plains zebra stallions.

Elephant family.

Governors' Camp balloon safari.

8   Olive baboon and young.

Male Maasai giraffe necking.

Hippo threat display.

Maasai herdsmen and cattle.

Lilac-breasted roller.

African wild dogs (also known as hunting dogs and Cape hunting dogs).

Female leopard at Mara Buffalo Rocks, Maasai Mara GR.

Toto, son of Honey, stars of *Big Cat Diary*.

Male lions, Selous GR, Tanzania.

Common wildebeest and calf.

Elephant matriarch.

Male defassa waterbuck.

Rothschild's giraffe, Giraffe Manor, Kenya.

African civet cat.

Maasai warrior and elder.

Female black rhino with red-billed oxpeckers.

Angola colobus, Chale Island, Kenya coast.

Maasai giraffe and calf.

Nairobi Elephant Orphanage.

Southern ground hornbill.

Common warthogs.

Jonathan and Angela with their cameras and laptops.

Spotted hyenas scent marking.

Lappet-faced vultures.

Chui the leopard (Bella's son), star of *Big Cat Diary*.

Maasai giraffe and newborn calf.

34   Plains zebras.

White Eye of the Marsh Pride, Maasai Mara GR, Kenya.

Grey crowned cranes.

Male cheetahs.

Klipspringer antelopes.

Male kori bustard displaying.

Spotted hyena and cubs.

Kike, star of *Big Cat Diary*.

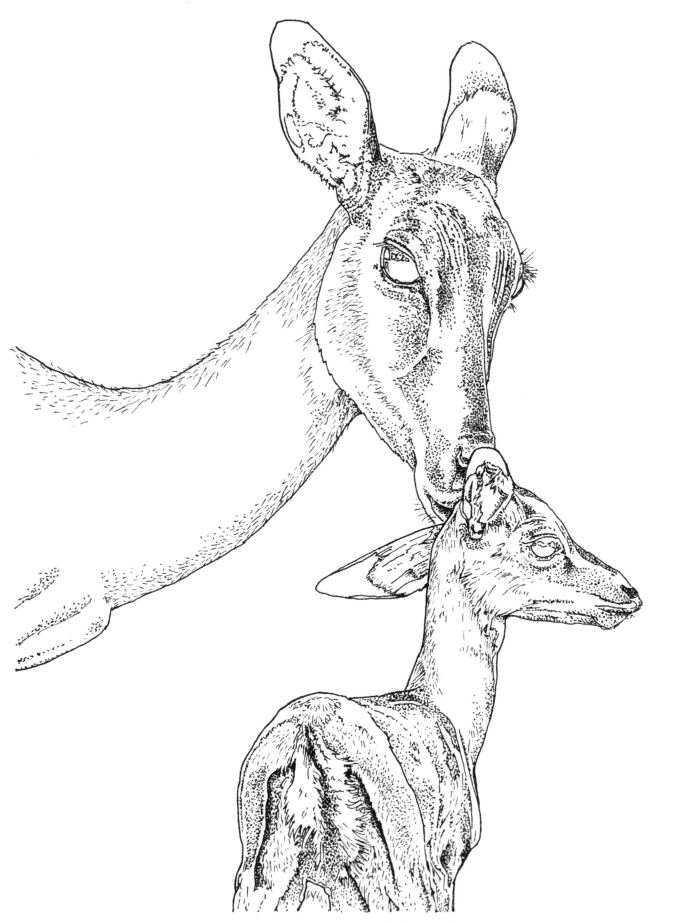

Impala and calf.

Common wildebeest on migration in Serengeti NP, Tanzania.

Maasai herdsmen.

Yearling African wild dog playing with puppy.

Half-Tail the leopard, star of *Big Cat Diary*, Maasai Mara GR, Kenya.

Topi antelope.

Scarface and lioness mating.

Martial eagles.

Leopard cubs at Mara Buffalo Rocks.

African buffalos.

Cheetah and cubs crossing the Mara River, Kenya.

Lioness carrying cub.

Captions

Established in 1964, the International Union for Conservation (IUCN) of Nature's Red List has seven levels of conservation representing different threat level: least concern, near threatened, vulnerable, endangered, critically endangered, extinct in the wild, and extinct. Species not threatened by extinction are placed within the first two categories – least concern and near-threatened. Those most threatened are placed within the next three categories – vulnerable, endangered, and critically endangered. Some 28% of all assessed species – +40,000 species – are threatened with extinction; loss of habitat and genetic variation being the primary causes.

Page 3: Lion and lioness. Males weigh around 180kg, lionesses 120kg. Males leave natal pride at two to three years of age forming a coalition with same-sex relatives. Sometimes non-related males form coalitions, as single males have little chance of winning a territory. Coalitions of four or more are always related. Population: 25,000. *Threat level: vulnerable*

Page 4: Male impala and herd of females. Males have horns. Impala can leap 3 metres high and 10 metres wide. Primarily grazers but browse on bushes in dry season. *Threat level: least concern*

Page 5: Plains zebra stallions. Social system based around a stallion and his harem. Males fight over possession of females. Population: 700,000. *Threat level: least concern*

Page 6: Elephant family. Population crashed from 1.2 million to 600,000 in the 1980s. Ivory is still a prized commodity in the Far East. Population: 415,000 savannah elephants. *Threat level: endangered*

Page 7: Governors' Camp balloon safari. Visitors to Maasai Mara GR can enjoy a balloon safari at sunrise, floating across the plains ending with a lavish bush breakfast and glass of bubbly.

Page 8: Olive baboon and young. Most wide-ranging of baboons, native to 25 African countries: Mali eastward to Ethiopia and Tanzania. Troops of 15 to 150 individuals, roosting at night in trees or rocky outcrops. Leopards sometimes kill baboons – and baboons sometimes kill leopards. *Threat level: least concern*

Page 9: Male Maasai giraffe necking. Bulls perform a ritualised form of fighting, swinging their neck and head to deliver powerful blows, helping to establish their place in male hierarchy. *Threat level: vulnerable*

Page 10: Hippo threat display. Hippo are grazers, leaving the river at dusk to forage. They can feel vulnerable on land and are said to kill more people in Africa than any other large herbivore. Lions sometimes attack hippo but are wary of a bite from their permanently growing canine tusks. Population: 115–130,000. *Threat level: vulnerable*

Page 11: Maasai herdsmen and cattle. The Maasai originate from the Nile region, moving south with their cattle in the 15th century and eventually settling in Kenya and Tanzania. Traditionally they followed the rains like their livestock, becoming more sedentary as their communally owned land was sub-divided into plots of 50–150 acres. They lived harmoniously with the wild animals rather than killing them for meat; consequently, some of the finest wildlife areas are in Maasailand. Population: 2 million.

Page 12: Lilac-breasted roller. Sub-Saharan Africa, preferring open woodland and savannah. Perches on tree stumps and bushes to "hawk" for insect prey taken on ground or in flight. *Threat level: least concern*

Page 13: African wild dogs (hunting dogs and Cape hunting dogs). Pack-hunting canines who run their prey to exhaustion. Unlike solitary cats, they lack a killing bite; instead they quickly disembowel and dismember prey. A dominant female gives birth annually to as many as to 12 puppies at a den. Pack helps provision pups by regurgitating food. Population: 6,600. *Threat level: critically endangered*

Page 14: Female leopard at Mara Buffalo Rocks, Maasai Mara GR. The most adaptable and widespread of the big cats: sub-Saharan Africa, parts of Middle East and Asia, including China, India, and eastern Russia. Hunts night or day; stores its kills in trees. Population: 100,000 in Africa. *Threat level: least concern*

Page 15: Toto, son of Honey, stars of *Big Cat Diary*. Up to 300 cheetah cubs are smuggled out of Africa each year to Yemen. Cheetahs fetch up to US$15,000 on the blackmarket across the Gulf States. *Threat level: vulnerable*

Page 16: Male lions, Selous GR, Tanzania. Lions have vanished from 95% of their historic range over past 100 years and are now extinct in 26 African countries. Tanzania has the largest population with 14,000 lions. *Threat level: vulnerable*

Page 17: Common wildebeest and calf. Some 500,000 calves are born January through March on the short grass plains of the Serengeti during rainy season; they gain their feet within five to ten minutes of birth. *Threat level: least concern*

Page 18: Elephant matriarch. An elephant family consists of a matriarch, her sisters, daughters and their calves. She is often the oldest and largest family member: a treasure trove of knowledge. They can live up to 60 years. *Threat level: endangered*

Page 19: Male defassa waterbuck. This large antelope is widespread in sub-Saharan Africa. Oily secretion acts as a water repellent for coat. Males have horns. Population: 95,000. *Threat level: near threatened*

Page 20: Rothschild's giraffe, Giraffe Manor, Kenya. Boutique hotel; guests pay a donation to the adjoining African Fund for Endangered Wildlife's Giraffe Centre. Their mission is to educate school children about their Rothschild's giraffe breeding programme and Kenya's incredible wildlife. Population: fewer than 2,500, 60% in Uganda. *Threat level: endangered*

Page 21: African civet cat. Large viverrid native to sub-Saharan Africa. Common and widely distributed in woodlands and secondary forests. Nocturnal, lives in tree hollows and among rocks. Feeds on carrion, rodents, birds, eggs, reptiles, frogs, crabs, insects, fruits and other vegetation. Civets are also found in tropical Asia. *Threat level: least concern*

Page 22: Maasai warrior and elder. Maasai warriors, their long hair smeared with red ochre, armed with spears and stabbing swords and carrying buffalo-hide shields, were greatly feared by the agricultural tribes. Their role was to protect their tribe and cattle, before settling down to marry and become elders.

Page 23: Female black rhino with red-billed oxpeckers. Rhino horn is a popular ingredient in traditional Chinese medicine, particularly in China and Vietnam. Demand in the Middle East nations (particularly Yemen) for ornately carved handles for ceremonial daggers (*jambiyas*) caused black rhino to decline 96% between 1970 and 1992. Population: 5,000. *Threat level: critically endangered*

Page 24: Angola colobus, Chale Island, Kenya coast. Found everywhere from the Congo Basin to Ruwenzori, Burundi and southwestern Uganda, as well as the montane and coastal forests of Kenya and Tanzania. Prized for their beautiful skins; their tails are used as fly whisks. Population unknown: between 3,000 and 5,000 in Kenya in 560–900 groups. *Threat level: critically endangered*

Page 25: Maasai giraffe and calf. There are four species of giraffe: Maasai, northern, reticulated and southern giraffe. There has been a 40% decline over the past 30 years owing to demand for meat and hides. Population: 68,000. *Threat level: vulnerable*

Page 26: Nairobi Elephant Orphanage. The Sheldrick Wildlife Trust's orphan elephant rescue and wildlife rehabilitation programme was founded in 1977 by Dame Daphne Sheldrick to honor her late husband, David Sheldrick, founder Warden of Tsavo, Kenya's largest national park.

Page 27: Southern ground hornbill. The largest hornbill, standing 1 metre tall. Ground-dwelling (unlike other hornbills), it feeds on insects, snakes, other birds, amphibians and tortoises. Among longest-lived of birds: 50–60 years (70 in captivity). Found across Kenya to South Africa, inhabiting woodlands and savannahs. *Threat level: vulnerable*

Page 28: Common warthogs. Large fleshy warts on the sides of their faces. Graze short grass on their knees and retreat underground at night reversing in to their burrows to ward off a pursuer with their sharp tusks. Lions sometimes dig them out and piglets are preyed on by big cats, hyenas, jackals and martial eagles. In decline over much of range. *Threat level: least concern*

Page 29: Jonathan and Angela with their cameras and laptops. They are based at Governors' Camp and have followed the Marsh Pride since 1977.

Page 30: Spotted hyenas scent marking. They live in clans, defending a territory marked with scent from their anal glands deposited on grass stems. Very vocal; long-distance whooping contact call. *Threat level: least concern*

Page 31: Lappet-faced vultures. The largest of 11 vulture species in Africa with a 2.1m wingspan, massive hooked bill and powerful feet. Folds of skin on neck are called lappets. Primarily scavengers. Vultures clean up 70% of Africa's carrion. Population declining owing to poisoning, persecution and ecosystem alterations. *Threat level: vulnerable*

Page 32: Chui the leopard (Bella's son), star of *Big Cat Diary*. The young male eventually left his mother to find a territory of his own. *Threat level: least concern*

Page 33: Maasai giraffe and newborn calf. Lions kill giraffe of all ages; hyenas occasionally take calves. They will defend their young with powerful kicks. *Threat level: vulnerable*

Page 34: Plains zebras. They wander widely in search of grass and water. Some 200,000 zebras migrate around the Mara-Serengeti annually. *Threat level: least concern*

Page 35: White Eye of the Marsh Pride, Maasai Mara GR, Kenya. Big cats survive on blood and body fluids from their prey during dry times and by hunting during cooler temperatures and at night. *Threat level: vulnerable*

Page 36: Grey crowned cranes. Approximately 1 metre (3.3 ft) tall, weighing 3.5kg (7.7 lbs), and with a wingspan of 2 metres (6.5 ft). Both sexes are similar, with males slightly larger. Breeding display involves dancing, bowing and jumping. Booming call, also makes a honking sound. Dry savannah, marshes, cultivated lands and grassy flatlands near rivers and lakes in sub-Saharan Africa. *Threat level: endangered*

Page 37: Male cheetahs. Solitary or in all-male coalitions, most commonly two to three litter mates that defend a territory against other males. *Threat level: vulnerable*

Page 38: Klipspringer antelopes. Typically nocturnal, primarily a browser, adults pair for life, territorial. Inhabit rocky terrain with sparse vegetation. Found across northeastern Sudan, Eritrea, Somaliland and Ethiopia to South Africa, and coastal Angola and Namibia. Population: 42,000. *Threat level: least concern*

Page 39: Male kori bustard displaying. Males weigh up to 19kg; heaviest flying birds in Africa. During breeding season they inflate their neck feathers and raise their white under-tail feathers. Nest is shallow hollow in the earth. *Threat level: near threatened*

Page 40: Spotted hyena and cubs. The most numerous large predator/scavenger in Mara-Serengeti: there are around 5,000 individuals in clans of up to 100 strong. Population: fewer than 50,000. *Threat level: least concern*

Page 41: Kike, star of *Big Cat Diary*. Only 7,100 cheetahs remain in Africa with perhaps 40 Asiatic cheetahs in Iran. Habitat loss, retaliatory killings by herders and illegal trade in cubs are the biggest threats. *Threat level: vulnerable*

Page 42: Impala and calf. Females live in herds of up to 100 in grassland and woodland areas close to water. Females hide their young in thickets for the first few days then join the nursery herd as predators find it more difficult to attack a group. Fawns suckle for four to six months. Population: 2 million. *Threat level: least concern*

Page 43: Common wildebeest on migration in Serengeti NP, Tanzania. Population: around 1.5 million including 1.3 million in the Mara-Serengeti ecosystem. *Threat level: least concern*

Page 44: Maasai herdsmen. Colourful ceremonies mark significant moments in Maasai culture: circumcision, warriorhood, marriage and elderhood.

Page 45: Yearling African wild dog playing with puppy. Pups first emerge from the den at three to four weeks. Hyenas and lions steal kills, and lions kill puppies when they start to move with adults. Rabies and distemper transmitted by domestic dogs can wipe out entire packs. *Threat level: critically endangered*

Page 46: Half-Tail the leopard, star of *Big Cat Diary*, Maasai Mara GR, Kenya. Killed in a wire snare in 1999 aged 11 while attempting to steal livestock from an enclosure at night. *Threat level: least concern*

Page 47: Topi antelope. A member of the hartebeest family often seen standing on termite mounds advertising their presence to rivals and keeping watch for danger. Plum-coloured thighs. Population: 70,000. *Threat level: vulnerable*

Page 48: Scarface and lioness mating. Scarface was part of a coalition of relatives, the four musketeers. He died aged 13 in 2019 after a long and successful reign in multiple prides. *Threat level: vulnerable*

Page 49: Martial eagles. Largest African eagle preying on guineafowl, gazelle fawns, warthog piglets, mongooses and monitor lizards. Pesticides and poison have caused a dramatic decline in birds of prey and vultures. *Threat level: endangered*

Page 50: Leopard cubs at Mara Buffalo Rocks. Two to three cubs are born at a den among rocky outcrops, thick bush or dead trees. Lions and spotted hyenas are a threat to cubs and adults. *Threat level: least concern*

Page 51: African buffalos. Bulls weigh up to a tonne and sometimes kill lions when attacked (small cubs not uncommonly horned and trampled). Population: 400,000. *Threat level: near threatened*

Page 52: Cheetah and cubs crossing the Mara River, Kenya. Females roam a home range of 35 to 1,000km² avoiding contact with other females. Jonathan and Angela are patrons of the Cheetah Conservation Fund (CCF). *Threat level: vulnerable*

Page 53: Lioness carrying cub. Up to four cubs are born at a secluded den. Young lionesses may be forced from their natal pride owing to competition for breeding sites and food. Lifespan: eight to 12 years for males, ten to 15 years for females. Bibi of the Marsh Pride was 17 when she was poisoned by pastoralists. *Threat level: vulnerable*

First edition published October 2022
Bradt Guides Ltd
31a High Street, Chesham, Buckinghamshire, HP5 1BW, England
www.bradtguides.com
Print edition published in the USA by The Globe Pequot Press Inc,
PO Box 480, Guilford, Connecticut 06437-0480

Illustrations copyright © 2022 Jonathan and Angela Scott

ISBN: 9781784778606
British Library Cataloguing in Publication Data
A catalogue record for this book is available from the British Library
Typeset and designed by David Scott
Production managed by Zenith Media; printed in the UK

SHARE YOUR CREATIONS WITH US!

We would love to see your finished artwork – tag us in your favourites on Instagram and Twitter via **@bradtguides** and we will share the most creative. Happy colouring!

Adding colour to your African safari

Grab your pencil crayons and embark on an African safari with the Big Cat People: award-winning wildlife artists and photographers, Jonathan and Angela Scott. Packed with birds and animals – including members of the Marsh Pride and many of the stars of the hugely popular TV series *Big Cat Diary* and *Big Cat Tales* – this colouring book with a difference is beautifully illustrated by Jonathan and Angela and also contains fascinating information about each species and its conservation status. Join them at Giraffe Manor and the Elephant Orphanage, or visit a tented camp and try a balloon safari – *The Safari Colouring Book* is both fun and thought-provoking.

Bradt GUIDES

51699
9 781784 778606

£9.99   US$16.99
bradtguides.com

Also available:

THE TRAVELLER'S COLOURING BOOK
A Journey Through Exceptional Places
Varvara Fomina

Bradt